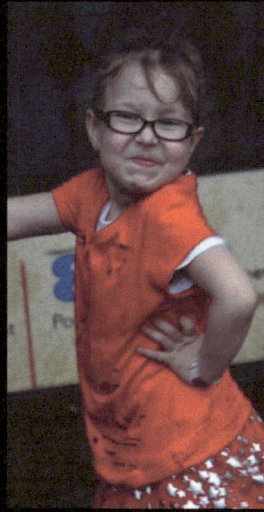

22Q at the Zoo

a 22Qtie Pie Book

MANDA JENKINS

Photography by

REBECCA RECK

ISBN 978-0692464090

First published in the United States 2015
by Betty and AL Books for Young Readers
16430 Hares Valley Road
Mapleton Depot, Pennsylvania 17052

First Edition

www.MandaJenkins.com

Dedicated to our 22Qtie Pie

~ Matthew Jacoby~

PITTSBURGH ZOO
& PPG AQUARIUM

Welcome to the zoo.

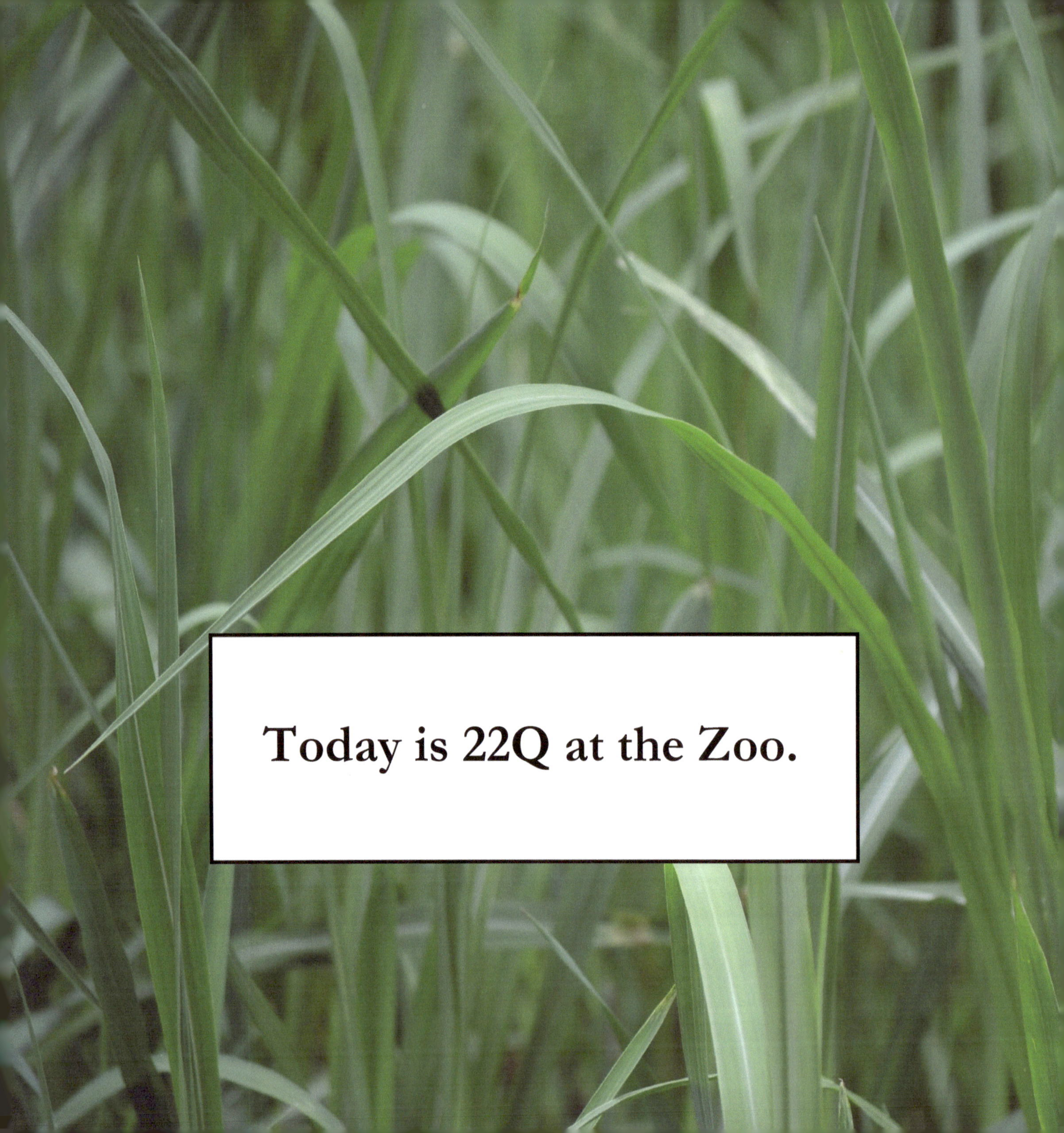

Today is 22Q at the Zoo.

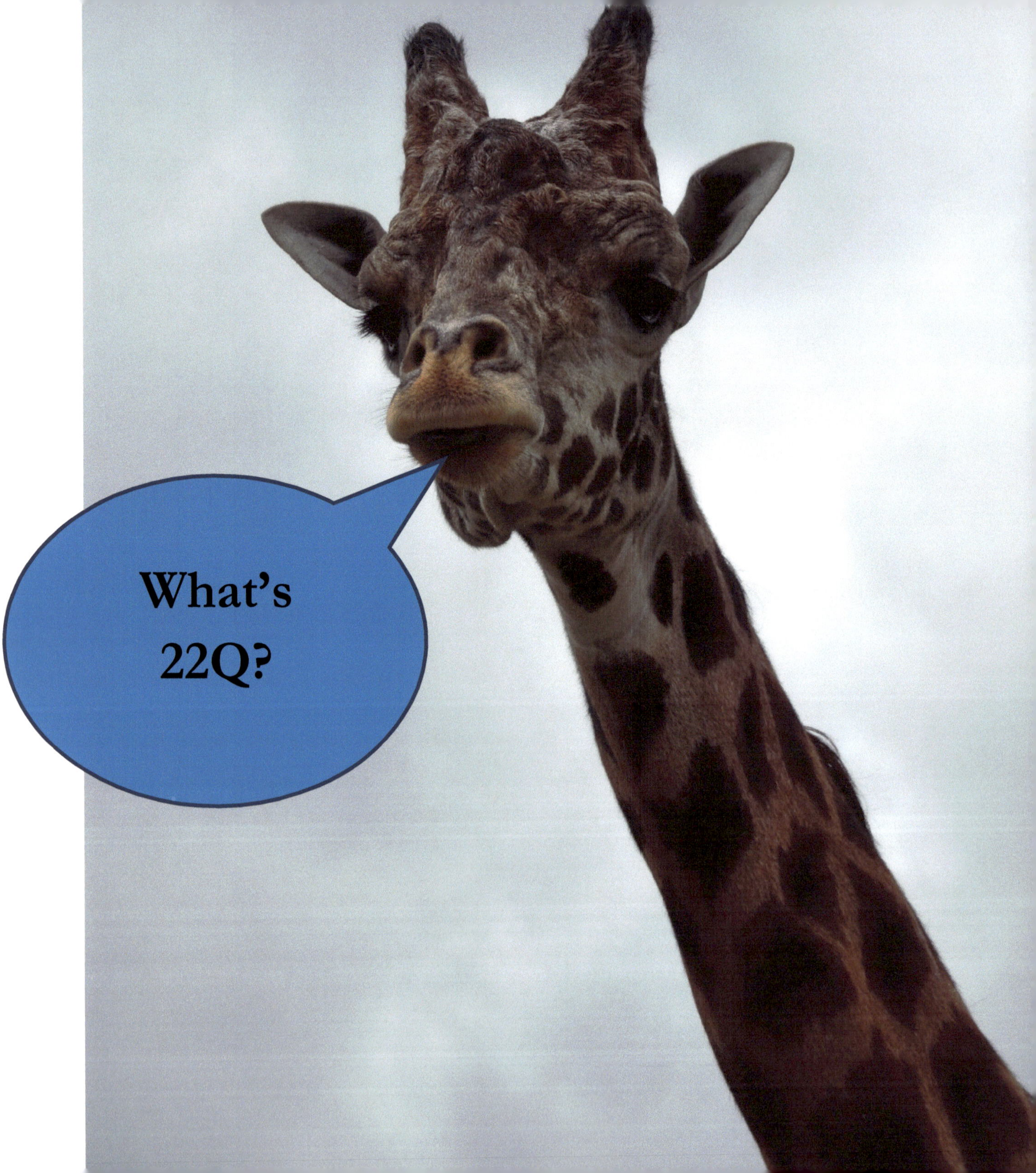
What's 22Q?

22Q is

22Q.11 Deletion Syndrome.

We love our 22Qtie Pies!

So every year

at zoos around the world,

we come together

for a day of fun.

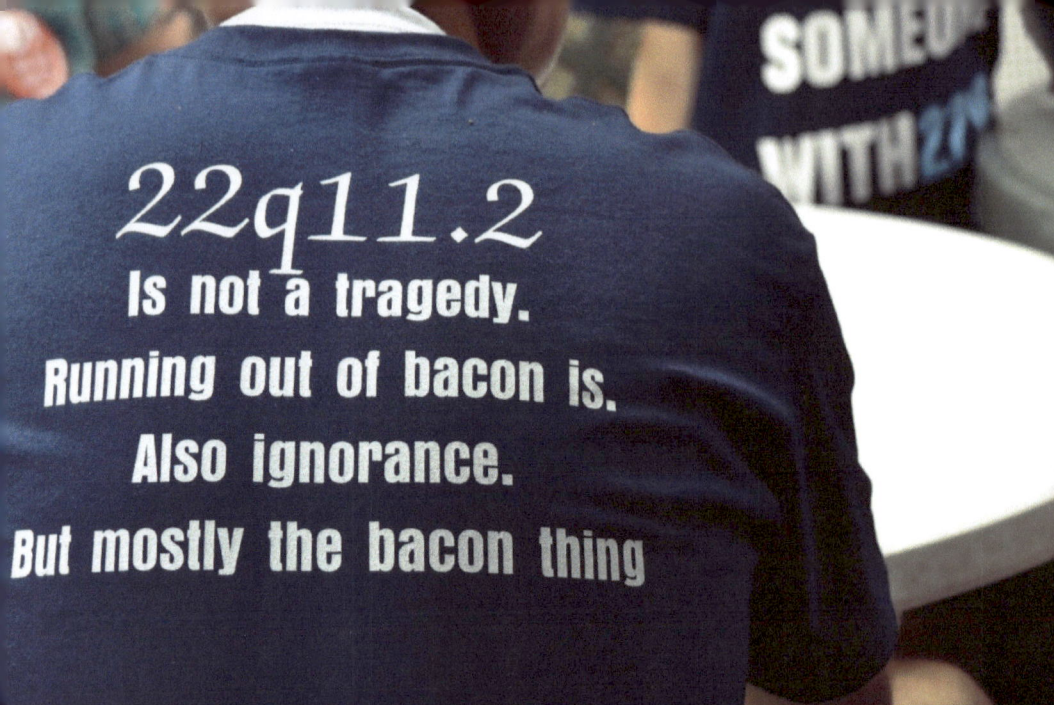

22q11.2
Is not a tragedy.
Running out of bacon is.
Also ignorance.
But mostly the bacon thing

SOMEO...
WITH 2...

WWW.22QBUS.COM

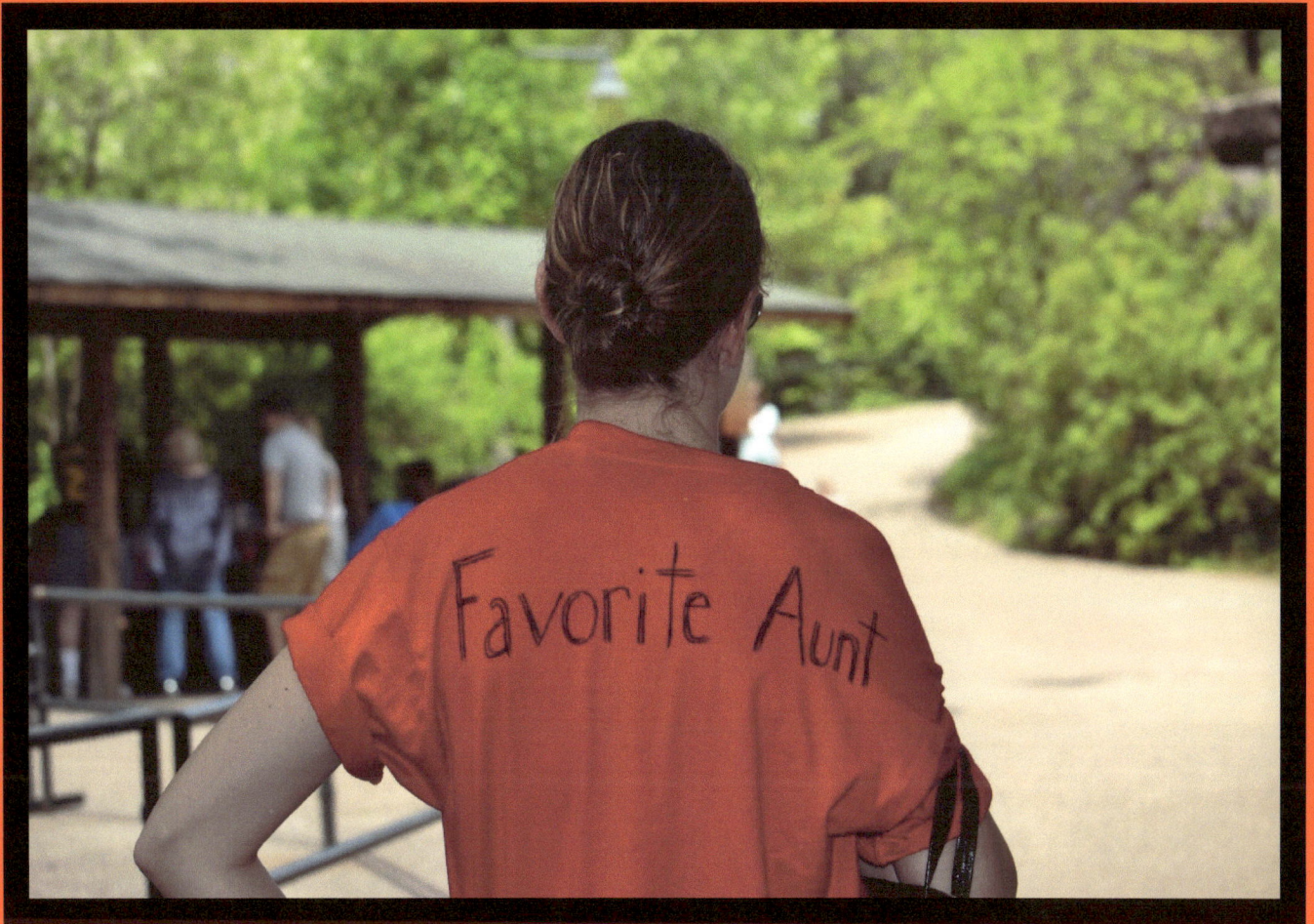

We wear 22Q shirts.

Hey gorilla!

Where is your 22Q shirt?

The Pittsburgh Area
22q
Family Support Network
Part of the International 22q11.2 Foundation Family Support Network

We talk to others about 22Q.

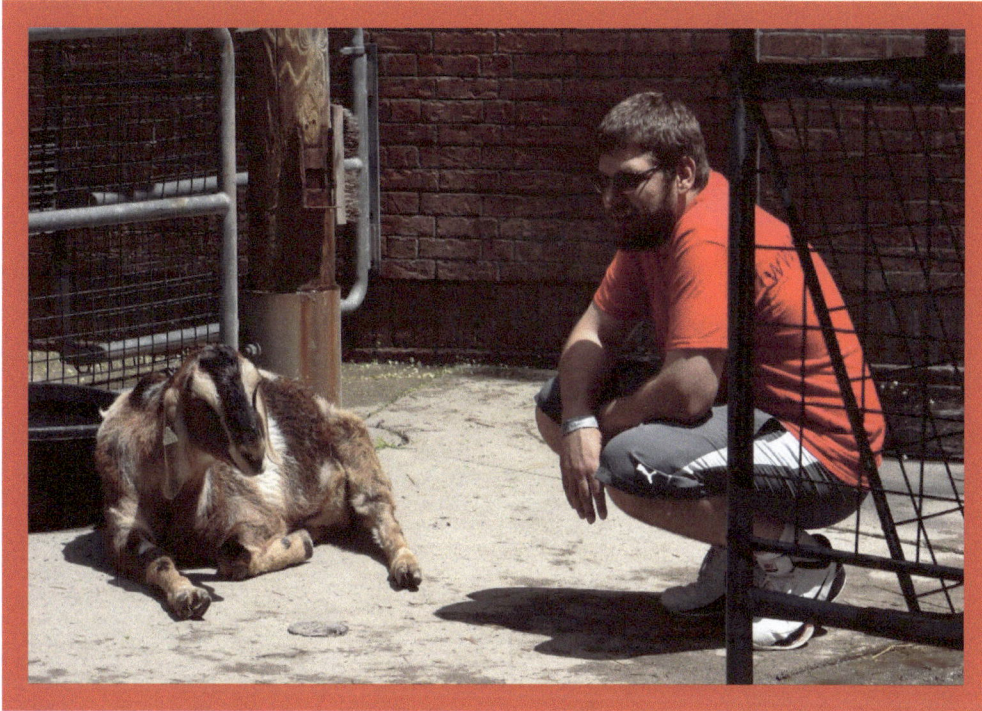

Even the animals listen.

We play at the zoo.

Penguins play too.

22Q at the Zoo

is BEARY fun.

Now it is time to rest for the next

22Q at the Zoo!

About 22Q.11 Deletion Syndrome

1. 22Q has also been known as DiGeorge, VeloCardio Facial Syndrome, VCFS, Opitz G/BBB Syndrome, and other names.
2. It is a genetic difference affecting about 1 in 4000 babies born every year and has no known cause for the microdeletion.
3. It is the 2nd most common genetic syndrome, following Down's Syndrome (affecting 1 in 400).
4. Each person with 22Q is unique, and the deletion can affect almost every body system.
5. Most have heart defects and feeding problems. Some have club feet, immune difficulties, and kidney dysfunction. Some don't seem to have any anomalies, yet others have dozens.
6. Genetic testing can now detect 22Q prenatally to prepare teams of specialists and families by birth.
7. There are wonderful resources for the 22Qmunity.
    a. The 22Q Foundation (www.22Q.org)
    b. The Dempster Family Foundation (www.dempsterfamilyfoundation.org)
    c. Children's hospitals around the world

www.ingramcontent.com/pod-product-compliance
Lightning Source LLC
Chambersburg PA
CBHW041238040426
42445CB00004B/65